exploring FRANCE

Peter Wickert

Contents

Unit 1	Where is France?	2
Unit 2	France, a varied country	4
Unit 3	Who are the French?	6
Unit 4	A place to live	10
Unit 5	Sun, snow and skiing	12
Unit 6	Butter mountains and wine lakes	16
Unit 7	Two contrasting regions	18
Unit 8	Coal and conservation	20
Unit 9	Paris – a world city	22
Unit 10	The sun and the sand of the South	26
Unit 11	Power for the people	28
Unit 12	Money matters	30

ONE

WHERE IS FRANCE?
Où est la France?

France and the European Community *La France et la Communauté Européenne*

France is one of the member countries of the **European Community** or EC. Twelve countries belong to this community (see Figure 1.1). Other countries in Europe may also join this community around the turn of the century.

TASK 1

1 Look at the traffic jam in Figure 1.2. Each of the cars has an identification plate saying which EC country they come from. Using the list of countries in Figure 1.1, try to work out which car belongs to which EC country.

2 Using an atlas and an outline map of Europe, name all the numbered countries in Figure 1.3. Mark in and name the capital city of each of the twelve countries.

3 Look at Figure 1.1. On the outline map of Europe that you used for question **2**, shade in the countries as follows:
(a) those who joined in 1957 – *ROUGE*,
(b) those who joined in 1973 – *BLEU*,
(c) those who joined in 1981 – *VERT*,
(d) those who joined after 1986 – *JAUNE*.
Fill in a key on your map. Write the colours in English.

What is the European Community? *La Communauté Européenne, qu'est-ce que c'est?*

The EC is a group of twelve countries, who have special **trading regulations** and who work as one unit. The main features of these trading regulations are shown in Figure 1.4.

EC Country	Year when the Country joined the EC
France	1957
West Germany	1957
Italy	1957
Luxembourg	1957
Netherlands	1957
Belgium	1957
UK	1973
Denmark	1973
Eire	1973
Greece	1981
Spain	1986
Portugal	1986
East Germany	1989

Figure 1.1

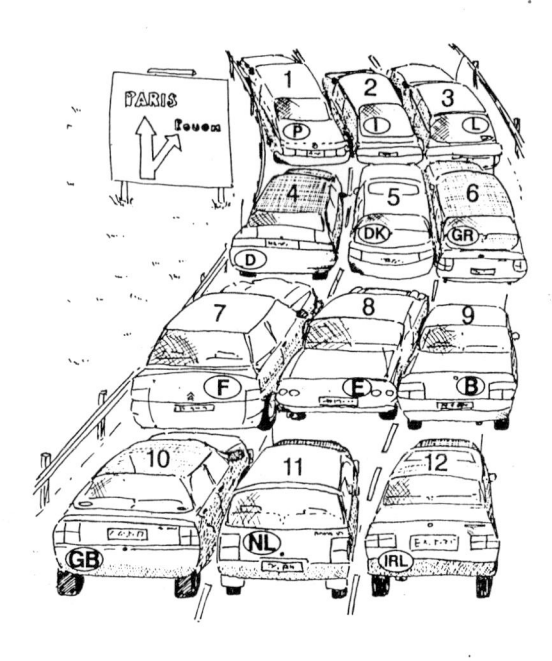

Figure 1.2

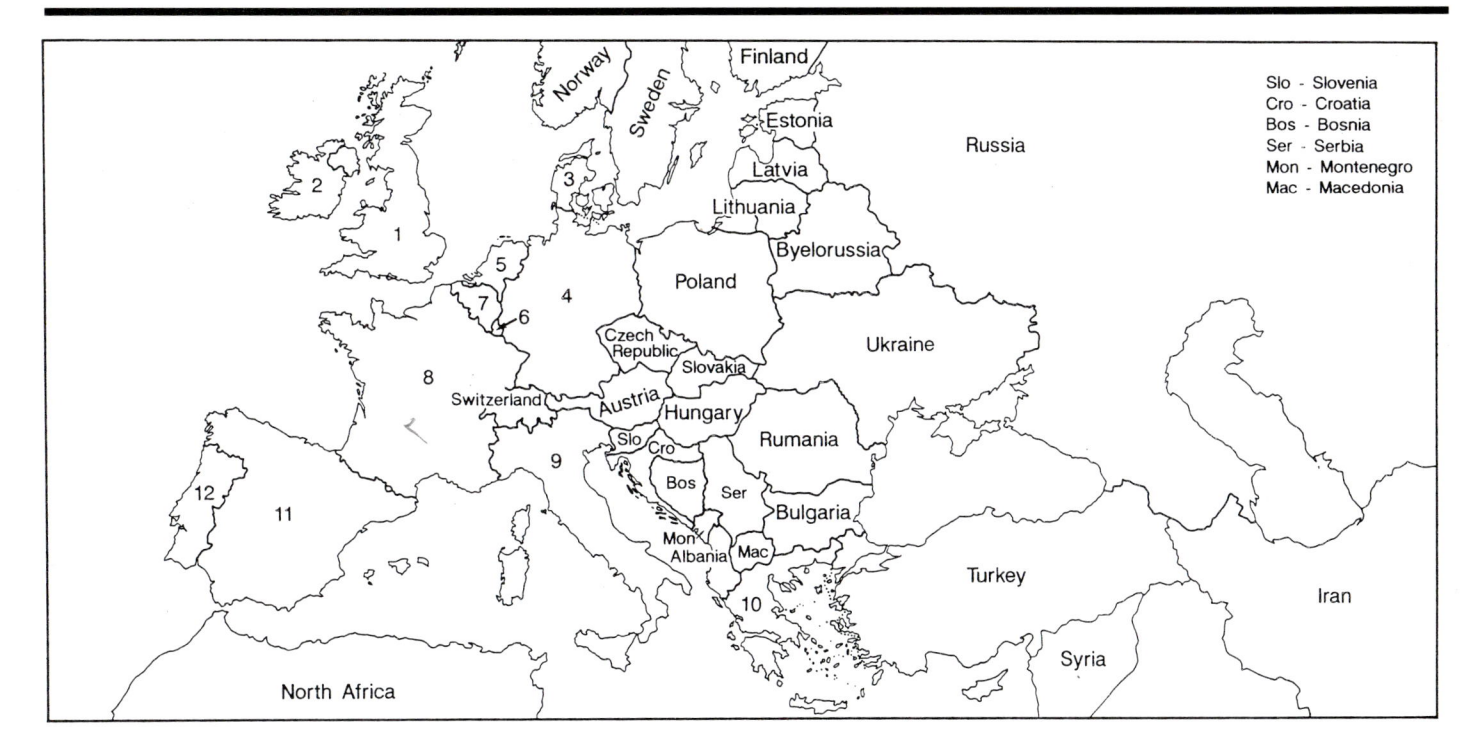

Figure 1.3

TASK 2

1 Do you think that all the ideas in Figure 1.4 are good ideas. Explain your answer.

2 Design a poster advertising the benefits of belonging to the EC.

VOCABULAIRE	
La Communauté Européenne	The European Community
La douane	Customs
L'Agence pour l'emploi	Job centre
La banque	Bank
Rouge	Red
Bleu	Blue
Vert	Green
Jaune	Yellow

Figure 1.4

1 A single European passport - You will be able to go anywhere in Europe with a single passport.

2 A single currency - The British pound, French franc and German mark for example, will be phased out and one single type of currency will be developed.

3 Equal job opportunities for all - Any person in any EC country will have the right to apply for a job in one of the other EC countries.

4 Few border controls - Passport control and border checks will be reduced and movement will be much quicker around the EC.

5 An elected government of EURO MP's (MEP's) - Every adult will be allowed to vote for a Member of the European Parliament to represent them.

6 A common farm policy - Farmers are guaranteed a price for the things they produce, and money is available for improving farms.

7 Financial help to develop the poorer areas within the community. For example, building a motorway.

TWO

FRANCE, A VARIED COUNTRY
La France, un pays bien varié

France is a large country, covering an area of about 547 000 sq km (just over twice the size of the UK). It has many different types of scenery (in French: *paysage*). In geography we call these different **physical landscapes** or **physical regions**.

TASK 1

1 Look at Figure 2.1. Using an atlas name the five areas of highland (**A**, **B**, **C**, **D** and **E**).

2 With the aid of an atlas and the French list in Figure 2.2, name the ten countries surrounding France, in French and English.

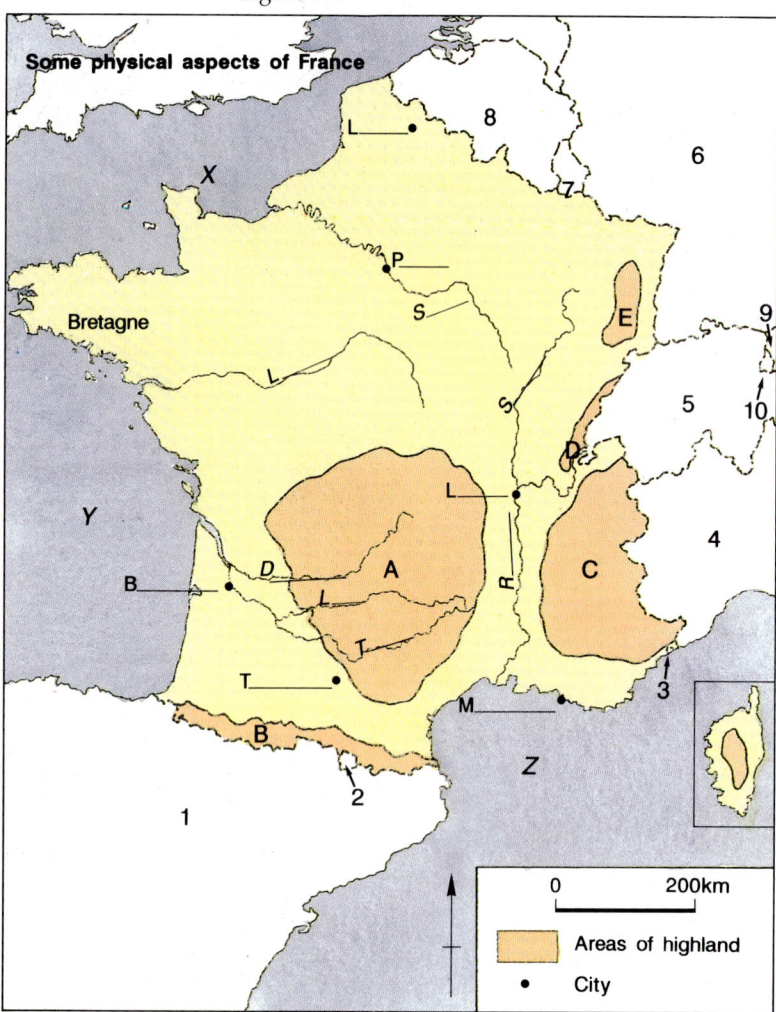

3 Name the sea areas **X**, **Y** and **Z**.

4 Name the seven rivers marked by their initial letters.

5 Name (**a**) the rivers which flow from the Massif Central,
(**b**) the river which flows through Paris,
(**c**) the river which flows southwards to a delta.

6 Why do you think Brittany (*Bretagne*) is important for fishing?

7 Name the six initialled cities marked with dots.

Figure 2.1

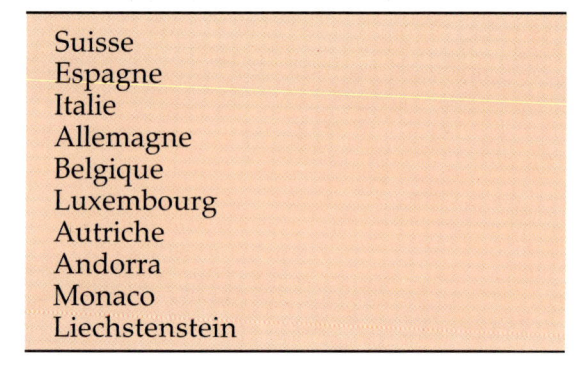

Suisse
Espagne
Italie
Allemagne
Belgique
Luxembourg
Autriche
Andorra
Monaco
Liechstenstein

Figure 2.2

The landscape can be divided into two main areas:
rural which means the countryside, and **urban** which means the built-up areas in towns and cities.

France has large rural areas where most of the land is used for farming and also large urban areas like Paris, which is the capital city of France and the seat of Government.

As France is such a large country it needed to be split up into smaller, more manageable areas. In 1982, the French Government divided up France into 22 **administrative regions** each with their own **local government** (see Figure 2.3). Each of these administrative regions are also divided into smaller areas called *départements*.

4

TASK 2

1 Look at Figure 2.3. Name three administrative regions in the south of France, three in the west, three in the north and three in the east.

2 Give three advantages of dividing France up into administrative regions.

So far we have looked at how the **French Government** has divided up France. However there are also many **natural landscapes** which define areas of the country.

Figure 2.3

TASK 3

Look at the photographs in Figure 2.4. They show a selection of French landscapes. Match up the letters of the photographs with the correct labels below.

1 The Massif Central: an area of high land which used to be old volcanoes.

2 The French Alps: an area of mountains. Now popular for winter sports and tourism.

3 The coast of Brittany (Bretagne): an area of fishing and farming villages where the local people speak the Breton language.

4 The Tarn Gorge: a deep limestone gorge cut by the River Tarn.

5 Le Midi (The South of France): sun, sand and beaches – the tourist paradise.

6 Beaujolais: famous for its vineyards.

7 The Somme: scene of many battles in the First World War.

Figure 2.4

VOCABULAIRE
Le paysage   Scenery/countryside
Bretagne   Brittany
Le Midi   The South of France

THREE

WHO ARE THE FRENCH?
Les Français, qui sont-ils?

The previous unit looked at how varied the French landscape is. Different types of landscape influence the types of jobs that people do – in other words **occupations** are related to **environment**.

TASK 1

Look at the list of French occupations in Figure 3.1 and match them up with the landscapes in Figure 3.2. You may feel that some of these have several possible answers. Write down the matching pairs which you think are most accurate and give reasons for your choice.

A mountain area

A large city

A small village

A forest

A coastal settlement

An area of fertile soil

Figure 3.2

TASK 2

Look at the descriptions of a selection of different French environments (Figure 3.3). Draw a table like the one which has been started (Figure 3.4) and list the environments in order of attractiveness. Put the most attractive at the top and the least attractive at the bottom. Fill in the rest of the table with what you think are the advantages and disadvantages of each environment.

Figure 3.1

Secondary school teacher

Car worker

Farmer

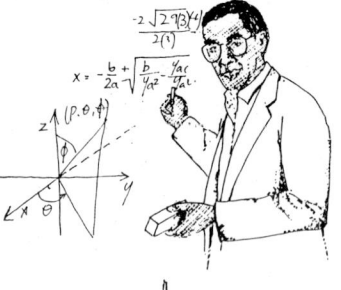

Office worker

Skiing instructor

Fisherman

The French Alps: tourist centre; poor farming.
Lyons: a large city; job opportunities; Densely populated.
The coast of western France: sandy beaches; coniferous forest.
The North of France: area of industry, some of it in decline; cheaper housing; some employment.
Beaujolais: area of vineyards and farming; mainly small villages.

Figure 3.3

| Rank | Environment | Advantages | Disadvantages |

Figure 3.4

As some areas **attract** and others **repel**, the French people choose to live in some areas and not in others – for example, many people choose to live in Paris. We call these areas **densely populated** areas. Places which repel people are called **underpopulated** areas, which means there are too few people living there. In some cases people move from one area to another – this is called **migration**. An already underpopulated area such as the Massif Central (see Figure 2.1 on page 4) is losing a lot of people because they are migrating or moving to other places. The Massif Central is said to be experiencing **depopulation**.

TASK 4

1 Trace a copy of the outline of France and its regions (Figure 3.6). Using the figures, shade in the map according to the following key:
−1.0 to   0.0 dark red
  0.0 to +1.0 light blue
  1.0 to +2.5 dark blue.

2 The map you have shaded is called a **choropleth map**. It should show you very quickly the pattern of movement of people in France – the regions where people are moving out (**migrating from**) and regions where people are moving in (**migrating to**). Give your map a title starting with the words 'A choropleth map showing . . .'

TASK 3

1 What is migration?

2 What does it mean if we say an area is densely populated? What problems do you think may occur if an area is densely populated?

3 Explain the term depopulation. Why is this bad for the Massif Central?

4 What is meant by the term an underpopulated area?

The French census
Le recensement Français

Almost all countries in the world hold a census (normally every ten years). A census is an official count of the number of people in a country. As well as lots of other information a census also gains information on family size, migration and occupations. Figure 3.5 is a summary of some of the main points of the census taken in 1991. This census also showed some interesting facts about where people wish to live in France. Figure 3.6 shows which regions in France had the greatest loss of people (negative numbers) and which regions had the greatest increase of people (positive numbers), between the years 1975 and 1990.

The 1991 French Census

Figure 3.5

Total population (including Corsica):	56 556 000
Increase in population since 1982:	2 220 000
Population Growth Rate: per year	0.5%

Figure 3.6

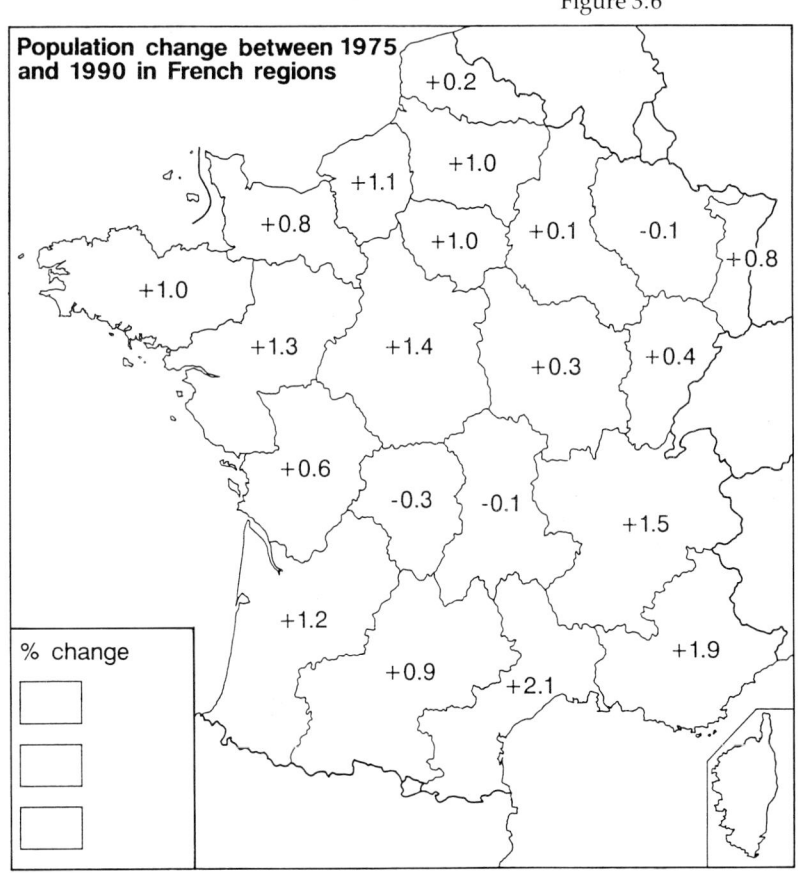

Population change between 1975 and 1990 in French regions

+0.2
+1.1 +1.0
+0.8 +1.0 +0.1 −0.1 +0.8
+1.0
+1.3 +1.4 +0.3 +0.4
+0.6
−0.3 −0.1 +1.5
+1.2
+0.9 +2.1 +1.9

% change

The Channel Tunnel and the TGV *Tunnel Transmanche et le TGV*

The Channel Tunnel or *Tunnel Transmanche*, opened in late 1993, has been built by a private company called Eurotunnel. This is the most expensive building project ever undertaken in Europe, costing nearly £10 billion. Figure 3.7 shows a cross section of the tunnel. The two main tunnels have a single line of track running in each direction from Cheriton (near Folkestone) to Sangatte (near Calais) (see Figure 3.8).

The tunnel is for trains only; cars and other road vehicles are transported with their passengers on the trains. Shuttles are expected to run every 12 minutes.

The French Government have built a new high speed railway line between the tunnel and Paris. Other connections to Brussels and Amsterdam are also planned. These trains will run at 297.6 km/h and are known as *Trains à Grande Vitesse (TGV)*. The journey from London to Paris will be just over three hours.

Cross-section of the Channel Tunnel

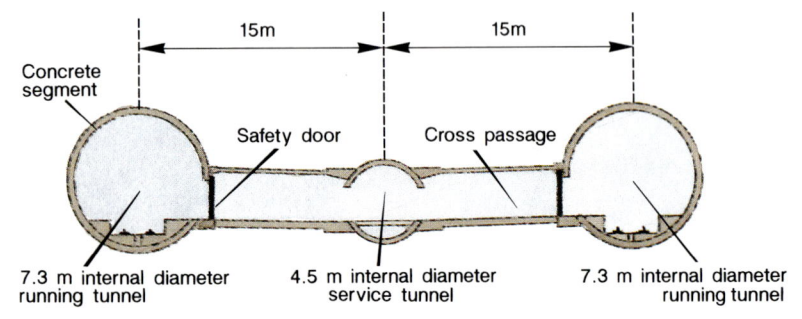

Figure 3.7

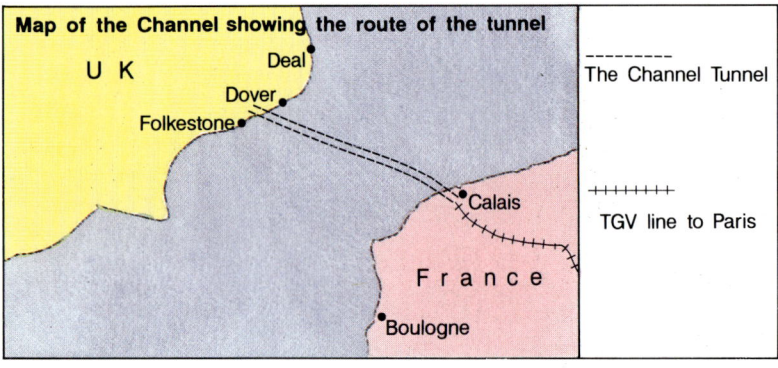

Figure 3.8

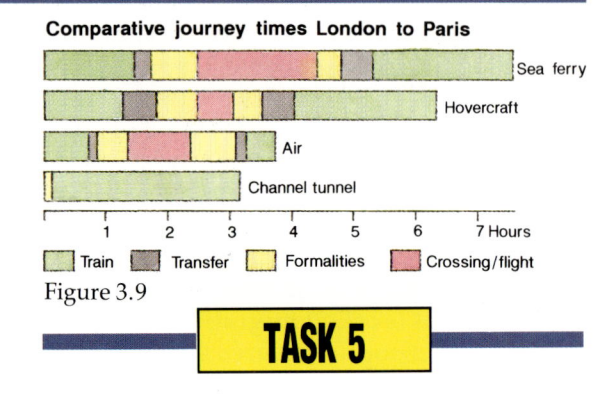

Figure 3.9

TASK 5

1 Look at the graphs in Figure 3.9.
(a) Which method of travel takes the longest time from London to Paris?
(b) By air is a very quick way to travel. How long does it take to get from London to Paris? How long is the flight? Why does it take longer than going via the Channel Tunnel?
(c) What effect do you think the Channel Tunnel may have on companies that operate ferries and hovercrafts?

2 Using a word processor write a letter to Eurotunnel asking them for a brochure and other information about the tunnel. Ask your teacher to post it for you. Using this information compile a short project about the tunnel, its history and its future. (The address of Eurotunnel is: Eurotunnel Exhibition Centre, St. Martins Plain, Cheriton High Street, Folkestone, Kent CT19 4QD).

Figure 3.11

The map (Figure 3.10) shows the area of Northern France which will be affected by the new tunnel. This region is called the Pas de Calais. It has, until recently, been a fairly poor part of France (especially when compared with Paris or the South of France), with old industries and fairly high unemployment. The Channel Tunnel and its connection to the UK should help to improve the wealth of the Pas de Calais.

Figure 3.10 *Map of Calais and Boulogne-Sur-Mer.*

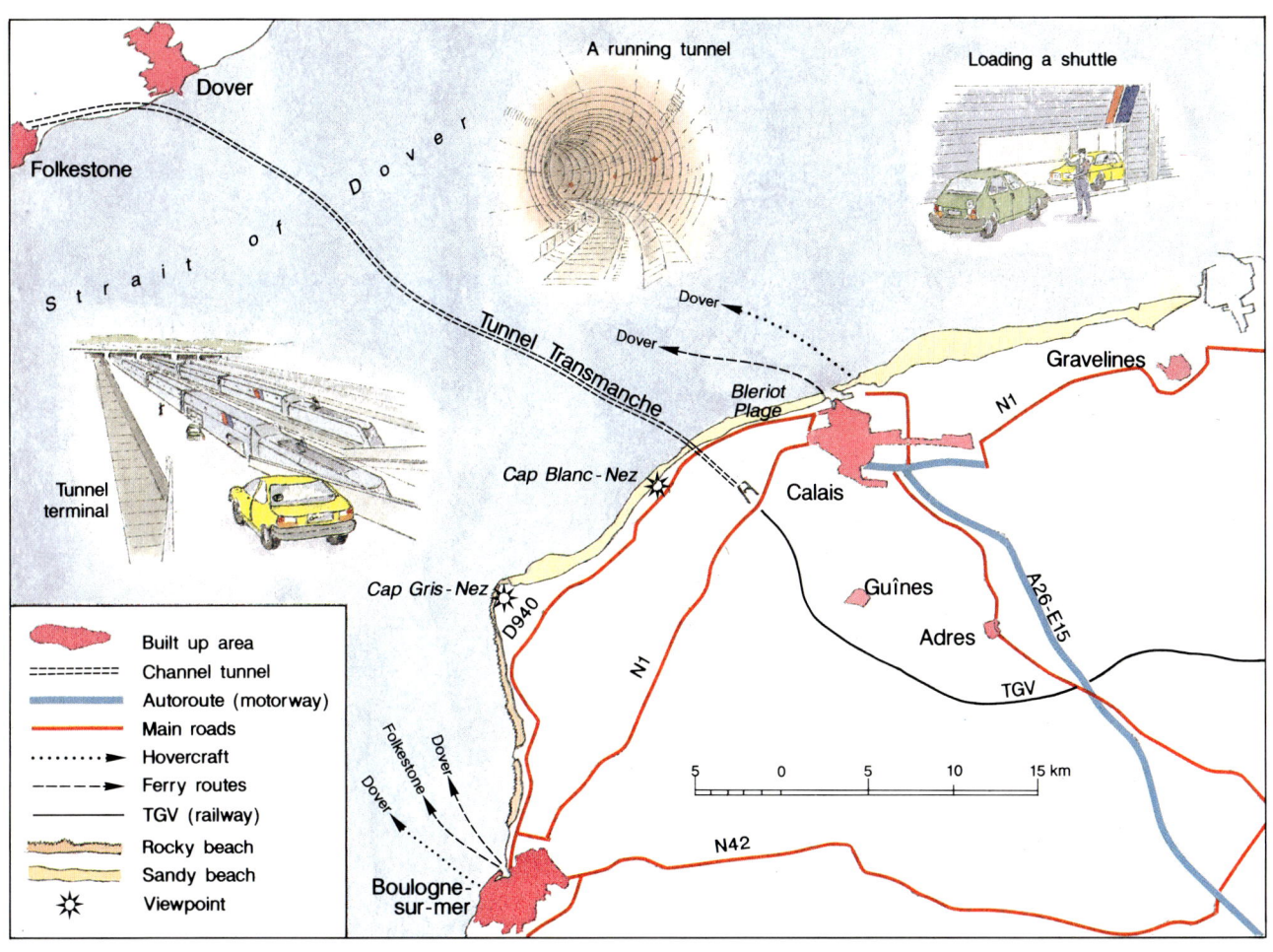

TASK 6

Look at the map (Figure 3.10) and answer the following questions.

1 Name the two main settlements on this part of the coast of France.

2 Main roads in France are known as *Routes Nationales* and are labelled with a capital N followed by a number. Name the Route Nationale which joins the two main settlements from question 1.

3 Calais connects with one port in the UK. Name the port.

4 Name the two British ports which connect by ferry to Boulogne-sur-Mer.

5 Name the two headlands found between Calais and Boulogne. What do the names mean in English?

6 What type of road is the A26-E15 which runs south-eastwards from Calais?

7 What type of coast would you find at Blériot Plage near Calais.

VOCABULAIRE	
La Manche	English Channel
Le train	Train
Vitesse	Speed
La plage	Beach
Gris	Grey
Le nez	Nose
Blanc	White

FOUR

A PLACE TO LIVE
Une habitation

A settlement is a dwelling or group of dwellings where people live. The decision where to site a settlement is based on many factors.

TASK 1

1 (a) Look at the list of French words in Figure 4.1. These are all important **resources** needed when living somewhere. However some of them are (i) more useful than others and (ii) used more often than others. In small groups decide which of the resources is the most important when choosing the site for a village. Give each of the resources a value from **1** to **5** with **5** being the most important and **1** being the least. These figures are called **weightings**.
(b) Now look at the map (Figure 4.2). Four suitable places for a settlement are labelled **A** to **D**. In your group discuss which lettered site is the best place for a village (you will need to consult the vocabulaire box for the meanings of the french words). Write the letter down and give reasons why you have chosen that site.

Figure 4.1

1 *L'eau*
2 *Le combustible (le bois)*
3 *Terre féconde*
4 *Matière de construire*
5 *Pâturage pour les animaux*
6 *Chasse*
7 *Pêche*

2 Now you can calculate whether you have chosen the most **economical** site, according to the values you placed on the resources in 1(a).
(a) Copy the table (Figure 4.3).
(b) Write your weighting for each word in the weighting column.
(c) For each settlement measure the distance in km from the lettered site to the nearest place where that particular resource will be found.
(d) Write the distances in each column for each lettered site.
(e) Distance can be shortened to the letter **d** and weighting can be shortened to the letters **wt**. In each column calculate **d × wt** and add up each column, putting the total in the box at the bottom. The most economical site for a village will be the one with the lowest score. How did your group do? Do you agree with the economical answer? If not give your reasons.

Figure 4.2

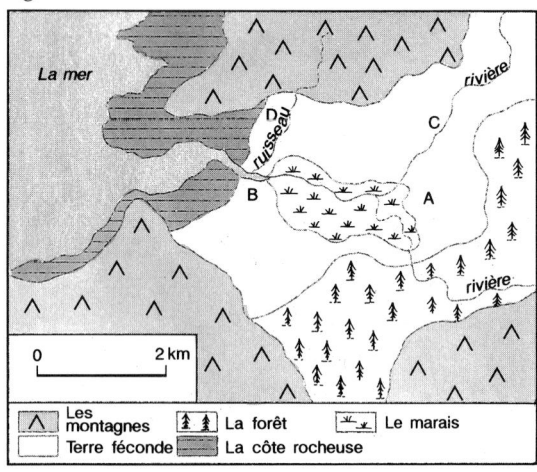

Figure 4.3

Resource	Weighting	Distance from A(km)	wt × d	Distance from B(km)	wt × d	Distance from C(km)	wt × d	Distance from D(km)	wt × d
1									
2									
3									
4									
5									
6									
7									
		Total		Total		Total		Total	

Some settlements are sited in narrow valleys (for example Chamonix mentioned in Unit 5, Task 2). The valley restricts the development of the town and it becomes a long thin settlement, known as a **linear settlement**.

Not only are French settlement shapes affected by the land surrounding them but they also have very different types of housing. This is often due to local building materials and climate.

TASK 2

1 Look at the photographs in Figure 4.5 and match them up with the areas shown in the key for the two maps (Figure 4.4).

2 Describe the main differences between the different types of house.

3 Use the French compass (Figure 4.6) to match up the features listed below with the right direction or region in France.

Roman tiles   L'Ouest (Bretagne)
Court farm   Le Nord
Bocage   A Paris

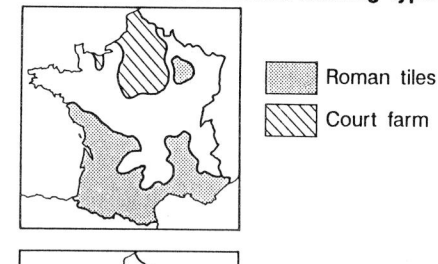

Figure 4.5

Figure 4.4

The distribution of French housing types

- Roman tiles
- Court farm
- Bocage (hedgerows and small fields)

Figure 4.6
French compass

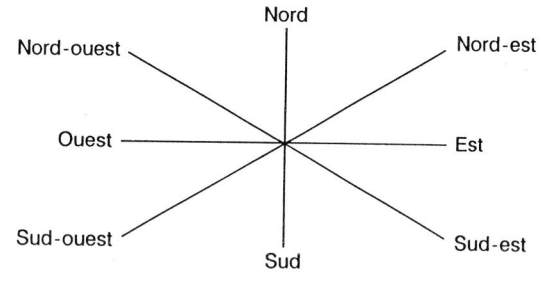

Nord / Nord-ouest / Nord-est / Ouest / Est / Sud-ouest / Sud-est / Sud

VOCABULAIRE

Le combustible	Fuel
Le bois	Wood
Fécond(e)	Fertile
Matière	Materials
Construire	to construct
Le pâturage	Pasture
La chasse	Hunting
La pêche	Fishing
Le marais	Marsh
Le ruisseau	Stream
Rocheuse	Rocky
Côte	Coast

SUN, SNOW AND SKIING
Le soleil, la neige et le ski

Tourism and recreation are a very important part of the French way of life. In 1990, 37 million tourists visited France – this is more than any other European country (see Figure 5.1). Paris alone attracts a great number of tourists – and tourists spend money which helps the economy of France. France can offer a great variety of tourist attractions.

TASK 1

1 Look at Figure 5.1. Arrange the countries into order of tourist numbers. Draw a histogram to illustrate the figures.

Figure 5.1

Number of tourists who visited a selection of EC countries in 1990

Country	Number of tourists (in millions) (1990)
Belgium	2.5
France	37
Germany	13
Greece	8
Ireland	3
Italy	26
Netherlands	3
Portugal	6
Spain	33
UK	15

2 Figure 5.2 shows the main method of transport used by tourists in order to get to France in 1990. Construct a pie chart to show these figures:
(Hint: Multiply each percentage by 3.6 to convert it to an angle – for example Road 60% becomes 60 × 3.6 = 216 degrees.)
Give your diagram a title with the words 'A pie chart showing . . .'

Figure 5.2

Main method of transport to France by tourists 1990

	Per cent
Road	60
Sea	13
Rail	12
Air	15

The French Alps
Les Alpes

Les Alpes are at the western edge of the European Alps. The highest point **Mont Blanc** (4248m) is found in Les Alpes near the skiing resort of Chamonix.

Les Alpes are a range of **fold mountains** formed over the last 10 million years. During the Ice Age the Alps were severely **eroded** by ice. Much of the ice has now disappeared. However, there are still large areas of ice in the form of **glaciers** to be seen, especially in the higher areas like Mont Blanc. A glacier is a very slow moving 'river' of ice (so slow moving that you would be unable to notice the movement), which gradually flows down a valley until it reaches warmer regions where it begins to melt – especially in the summer. Of course in the winter, the French Alps and the valleys are covered in snow and **winter sports** are an important tourist attraction.

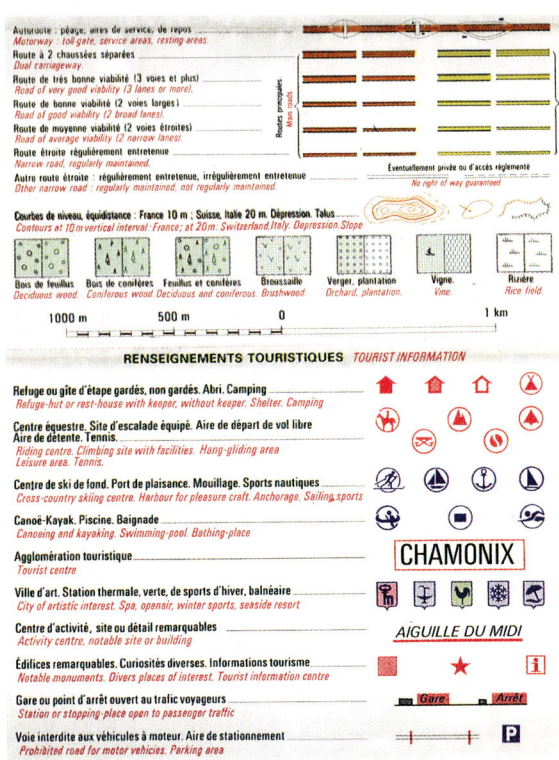

Figure 5.3

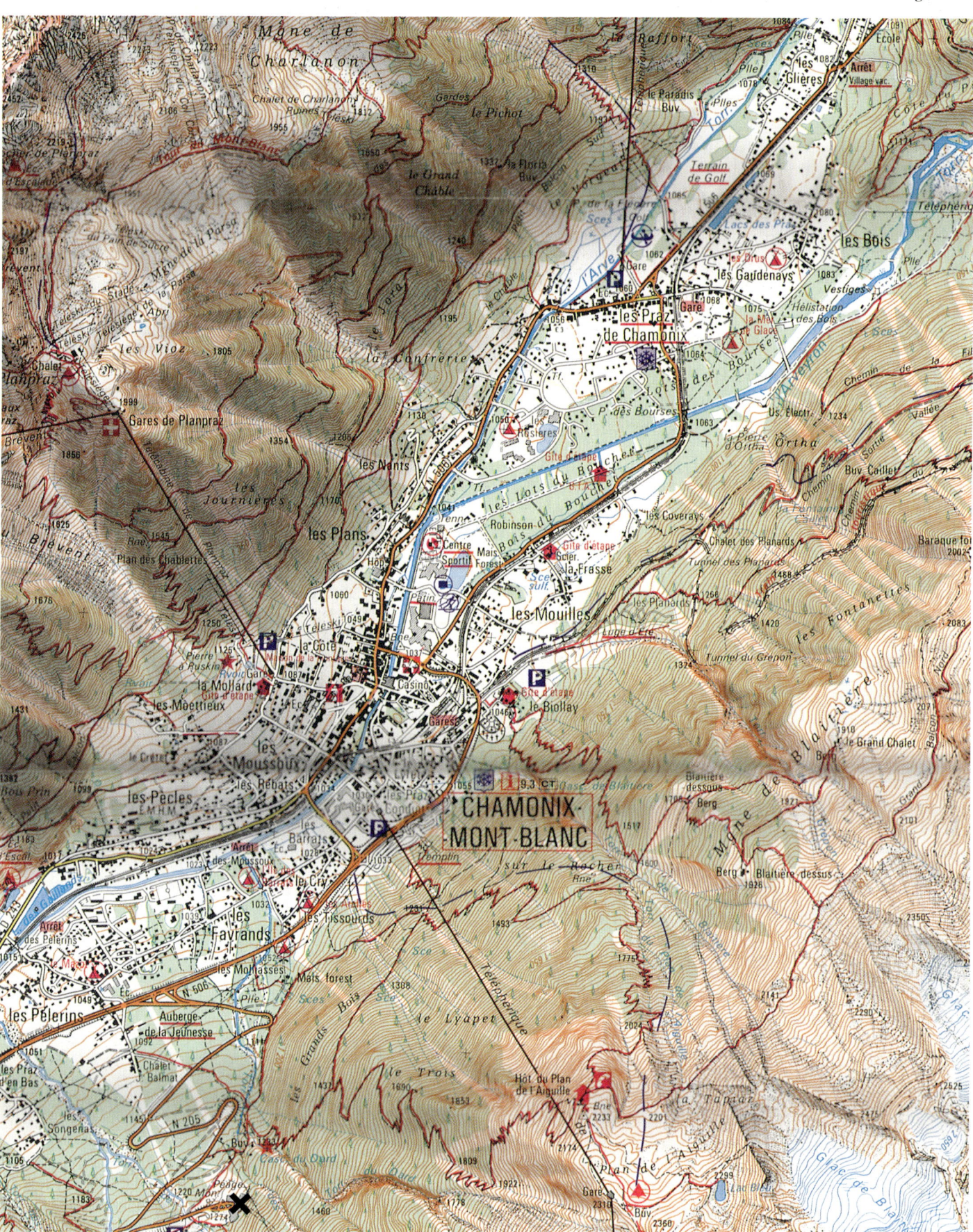

Reproduced by kind permission of L'Institut Géographique National

Conflicting issues in the French Alps

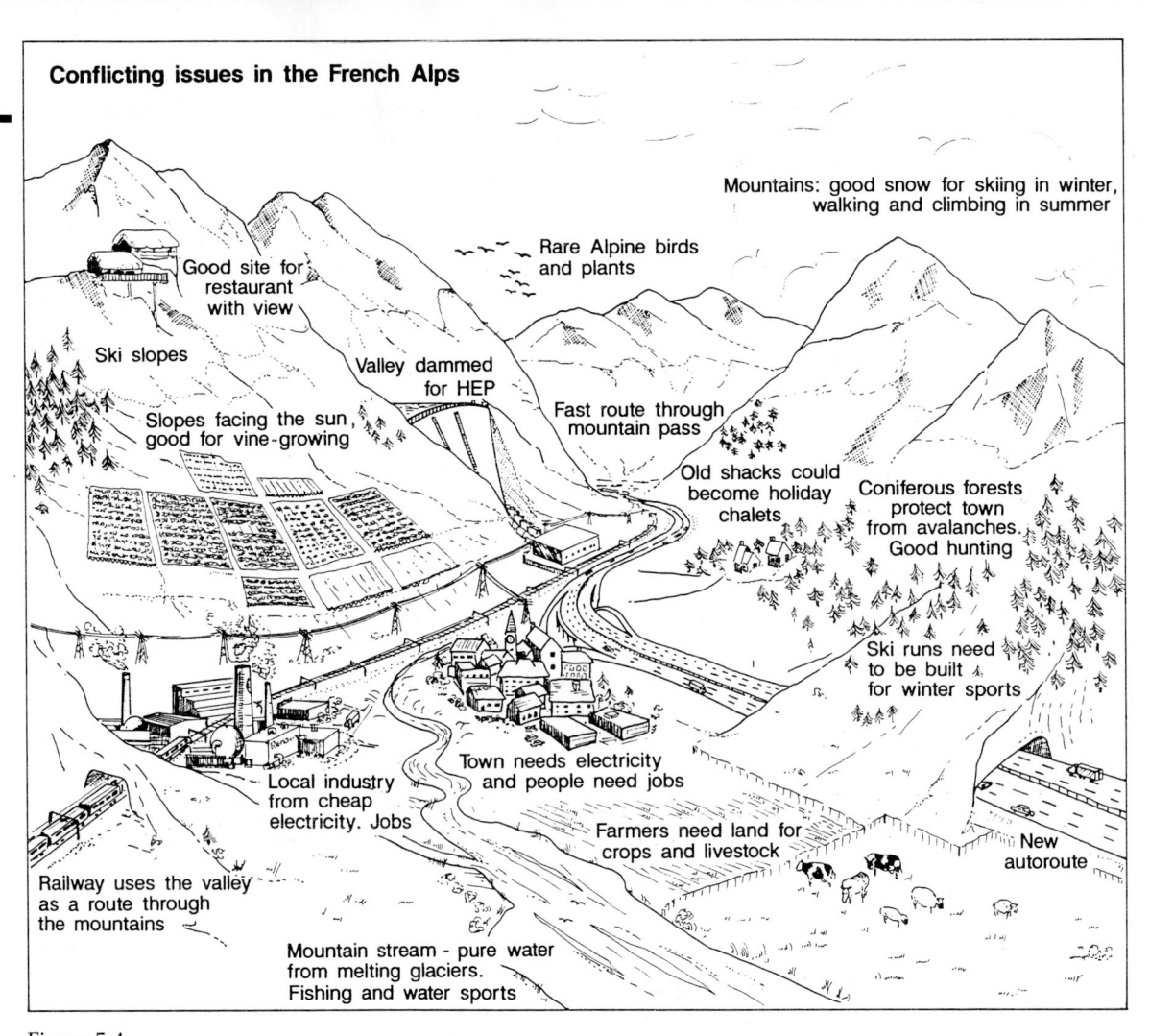

- Good site for restaurant with view
- Ski slopes
- Slopes facing the sun, good for vine-growing
- Rare Alpine birds and plants
- Valley dammed for HEP
- Mountains: good snow for skiing in winter, walking and climbing in summer
- Fast route through mountain pass
- Old shacks could become holiday chalets
- Coniferous forests protect town from avalanches. Good hunting
- Ski runs need to be built for winter sports
- Local industry from cheap electricity. Jobs
- Town needs electricity and people need jobs
- Farmers need land for crops and livestock
- New autoroute
- Railway uses the valley as a route through the mountains
- Mountain stream - pure water from melting glaciers. Fishing and water sports

Figure 5.4

Potential conflicts:

	Advantages	Disadvantages
Skiing	Encourages tourism Brings in money	Forests need to be cut down Soil erosion Ski lifts unsightly
Walking	Encourages tourism	Footpath erosion Some dangerous areas
Forestry	Protects slopes Protects against avalanches Land in fuller use Timber sales Hunting	Not as much money made from land
New autoroutes	Quick access to valley Safer roads Uses less petrol	Unsightly Noise and air pollution Brings in too many people Some people drive straight past
Industry	Employment develops the area	Air and noise pollution Unsightly
HEP	Cheap renewable electricity Environmentally acceptable Lake attractive Water sports	Expensive to build Areas need to be flooded Low employment
Mountain stream	Water needed for town, agriculture, tourism and industry	Easily polluted by all the above land uses

TASK 2

1 Look at Figure 5.3 (page 13), it is a detailed map of the area around Chamonix.
a) Using the key find out the number of the N road *Route Nationale* which runs through Chamonix. What direction does the road take across the map?
b) Chamonix is situated in a valley. How can we tell this from the map?
c) Why is Chamonix situated in the valley? Give at least four reasons.
d) How has the valley influenced the shape of the settlement?
e) The point marked **X** on the map is the entrance to the Mont Blanc Tunnel (11km long). From this point the tunnel runs due south east. Use an atlas to find out which country the tunnel leads to.
f) Which N road leads to the tunnel? Describe its route. Why does it take a route such as this?
g) Name three activities found on the map which would tell us that Chamonix is an attractive place for tourism.

2 a) Tourism certainly brings money into an area. However it can also bring some problems with it. In groups of three, discuss the sorts of problems that tourism can create. Note down your ideas and report them back to the class.
b) Using the information that you have gained from the previous question, design a poster telling tourists about the problems that they may bring to the area and what should be done to reduce the problems.

As well as tourists being interested in this area there are many other people who use the land (e.g. farmers, industry and road builders). This means that there are all sorts of **conflicting issues** about the use of this land. Figure 5.4 illustrates some of these conflicting issues.

TASK 3

1 Write a description in the style of a newspaper article describing the conflicting issues which can be found in *Les Alpes*.

2 Imagine that you have been appointed to manage this area – to get the most out of the area without destroying the natural landscape. Using all the information you have gained, taking into account all the different people who benefit from this region, work out what you think is the best plan to develop the area successfully. You should organise your ideas under the following headings: **1** TOURISM, **2** FORESTRY, **3** FARMING, **4** THE LOCAL POPULATION, **5** INDUSTRY and JOBS, **6** ROADS and RAILWAYS, **7** PRESERVING the NATURAL LANDSCAPE. What you have created is known as a **management plan.** Give your work the title 'My Management Plan for Les Alpes around Chamonix'.

SIX

BUTTER MOUNTAINS AND WINE LAKES
Les montagnes de beurre et les lacs de vin

Agriculture or farming is a very important **primary industry** in France. Agriculture can be divided into two main groups: a) **pastoral farming** (livestock) and b) **arable farming** (crops).

TASK 1

Look at the French list of items grown on a farm (Figure 6.1). In pairs find out what they mean and arrange them into arable and pastoral farming. In rough, divide your two lists further, into what you feel are suitable sub-groups (e.g. fruit, cereals). Note down your final decision and explain why you have decided on your sub-groups.

France has the largest area of farmland and is the largest producer of food in the EC. France is also one of the world's largest exporters of food. The agriculture is quite **diverse** – in other words it grows a lot of different things. This is mainly due to the different types of climate which can be found in France. The map in Figure 6.2 shows the different types of farming found in France.

Figure 6.2

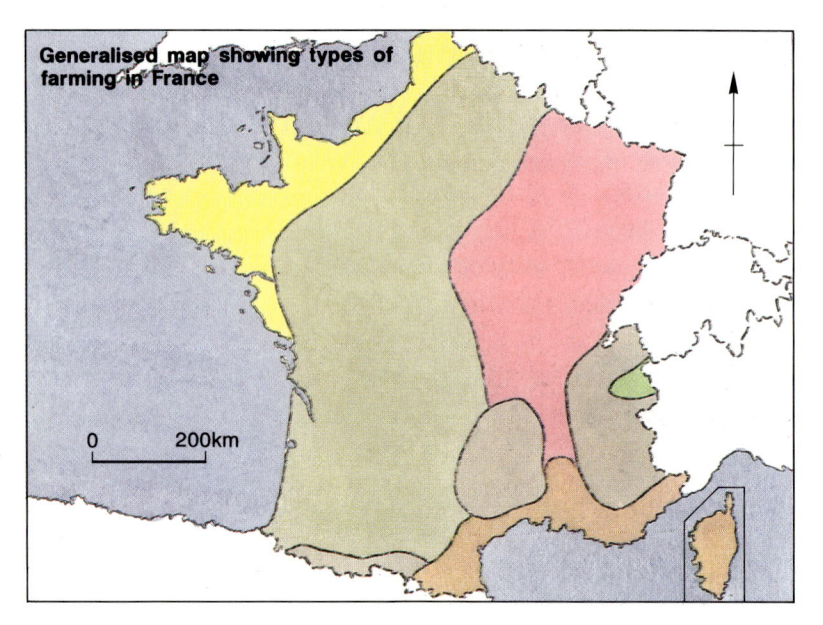

Figure 6.1

Les pommes	Le thé
L'orge	Les tomates
Riz	Les poires
Les Bananes	Le seigle
Les pommes de terre	Le café
Le pamplemousse	Les raisins
Le maïs	Le froment
Les moutons	Le coton
Les mangues	Les olives
Les oranges	Le colza
Les cochons	Les chèvres

The Common Agricultural Policy
La Politique Agriculturelle Commune

As you already know France is a member of the EC (see Unit 1). When the EC was set up in 1957 under the Treaty of Rome, agriculture was regarded as a very important part of the whole community for several reasons (see Figure 6.3). As a result the Common Agricultural Policy or CAP was set up to deal with farming in the EC. The CAP had several aims (see Figure 6.4).

Without doubt the CAP has achieved a great deal since 1957 but there are still many problems.

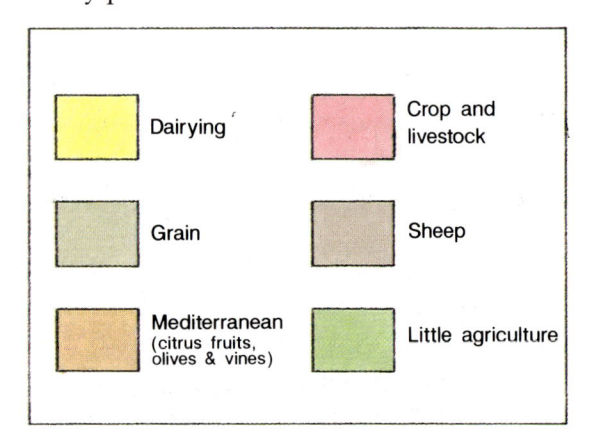

Generalised map showing types of farming in France

- Dairying
- Crop and livestock
- Grain
- Sheep
- Mediterranean (citrus fruits, olives & vines)
- Little agriculture

Figure 6.3

Reasons for setting up the Common Agricultural Policy

1 Fewer people were needed to be employed in farming because machinery was now being used more.

2 Many of the workers who lost jobs in farming would be used to develop French industry after the Second World War.

3 With even fewer people working on farms, agriculture would still have to supply food to France as it gained wealth from industry.

Figure 6.4

The aims of the CAP

1 To increase the amount of food produced by farms.

2 To make sure that farmers had a fair standard of living.

3 To make sure prices people paid for the food were reasonable.

4 To keep prices and amounts produced steady.

Butter Mountains and Wine Lakes

One of the main problems resulting from the CAP is the fact that, in some cases, too much food has been produced. This means that some products have to be stored until a later date, when they can be sold. These large stores of foods and liquids are called **mountains** and **lakes**.

TASK 2

1 What do you understand by the terms 'butter mountain' and 'wine lake'?

2 Read the letter concerning the Common Agricultural Policy (see Figure 6.5). Divide your page up into two columns and note down the advantages and disadvantages of the CAP.

3 Do you think that the CAP has been a good idea? Give reasons for your answer.

Figure 6.5

Dear Jean,

My research has come up with the following points regarding the CAP. The Common Agricultural Policy has reduced costs and made imports more reliable. Farmers are now better off and poorer farmers have been able to gain extra money by working in nearby factories or from tourism, but some would argue that these farmers spend less time on their farms. Whilst food surpluses (the so-called "butter mountains" and "wine lakes") have meant that a lot of food has been wasted, Europe has become more able to look after itself without importing from other countries. In any case, a surplus can be saved for next year to offset a possible crop failure. However, some food prices have increased and some areas further away from the centre of the EC have not gained as much wealth as the farms at the centre, although these farms would probably have gone out of business anyway. Farms have increased in size to the recommended level and the average field size is now bigger but a lot of hedgerows have been destroyed to do this. As a result wildlife has suffered and soil erosion has increased. Some industrial countries like the U.K. have objected to the high level of EC money (70%) spent on agriculture and feel that more money should be spent on other things like industry. I hope this is the information you require.

Yours sincerely,

VOCABULAIRE

Le maïs	Maize
La pomme	Apple
Le café	Coffee
La chèvre	Goat
L'orge	Barley
Le seigle	Rye
Le mouton	Sheep
La tomate	Tomato
Le riz	Rice
Le raisin	Grape
L'orange	Orange
La banane	Banana
La poire	Pear
La mangue	Mango
Le froment	Wheat
La pomme de terre	Potato
Le coton	Cotton
Le thé	Tea
L'olive	Olive
Le colza	Rapeseed
Le pamplemousse	Grapefruit

TWO CONTRASTING REGIONS
Deux régions bien différentes

Brittany
La Bretagne

Bretagne or Brittany is a **peninsula** in the north west of France. It is a very distinct region of hedgerows, small woodlands, small fields and villages. This type of landscape is called *Bocage* (see unit 4 for map). Bretagne also has a rocky coastline with little fishing villages and towns (see Figure 7.3). Its climate is fairly mild and wet (see Figure 7.1) due to the fact that the sea is never very far away – it is surrounded by ocean on three sides. In fact the region is so distinct that it even has its own language known as *breton* which is more similar to Cornish than French.

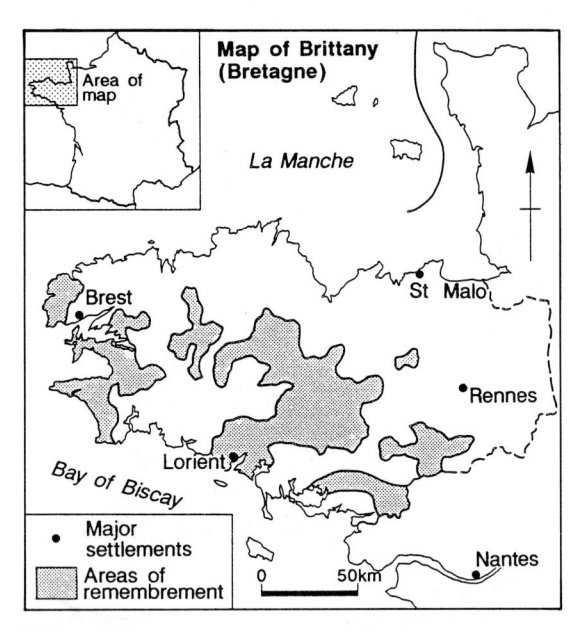

Figure 7.2

Figure 7.1 Temperature and rainfall figures for Brest

	J	F	M	A	M	J	J	A	S	O	N	D
Temp (°C)	7	7	8	11	13	16	17	18	16	13	10	8
Rainfall (mm)	88	75	63	63	48	50	50	55	58	90	105	110

Figure 7.3

TASK 1

1 Look at Figure 7.1. Which months have a) the highest temperature and b) the lowest temperature?

2 Which months have a) the lowest rainfall and b) the highest rainfall?

3 Construct a temperature and rainfall graph for Brest.

4 Calculate the total annual rainfall and the mean annual range of temperature (the difference between the highest and lowest figure).

5 What is the average rainfall per month. Draw a line across your graph to show this. How many months are above average and how many are below average?

The Massif Central

Just south of the centre of France is an area of uplands known as the Massif Central (see Figure 7.4). These uplands covering about 15 per cent of France were formed millions of years ago and consist mainly of hard rocks. Some of the rocks are actually the remains of old extinct volcanoes. At Le Puy a church is built on the top of an old volcanic plug (the hard rock in the central vent), these old volcanic plugs are known as **puys** (see Figure 7.5).

Figure 7.5

Industrial decline

Several coalfields exist in the Massif Central. However, coalmining has now stopped, mainly due to the difficulty of mining the coal and the lessening need for this fuel in the modern day. Attempts have been made to develop other forms of employment. One important industry is the **Michelin** rubber factory at Clermont-Ferrand famous for its tyres.

TASK 2

1 How many rocktypes can be found in the Massif Central? Which rocktype covers the largest area of the Massif Central?

2 Look at the ideas to combat rural depopulation (Figure 7.6). In pairs take each idea in turn and note down whether you think it is a good way of keeping the younger people in the area. Can you think of any other ways in which rural depopulation could be stopped?

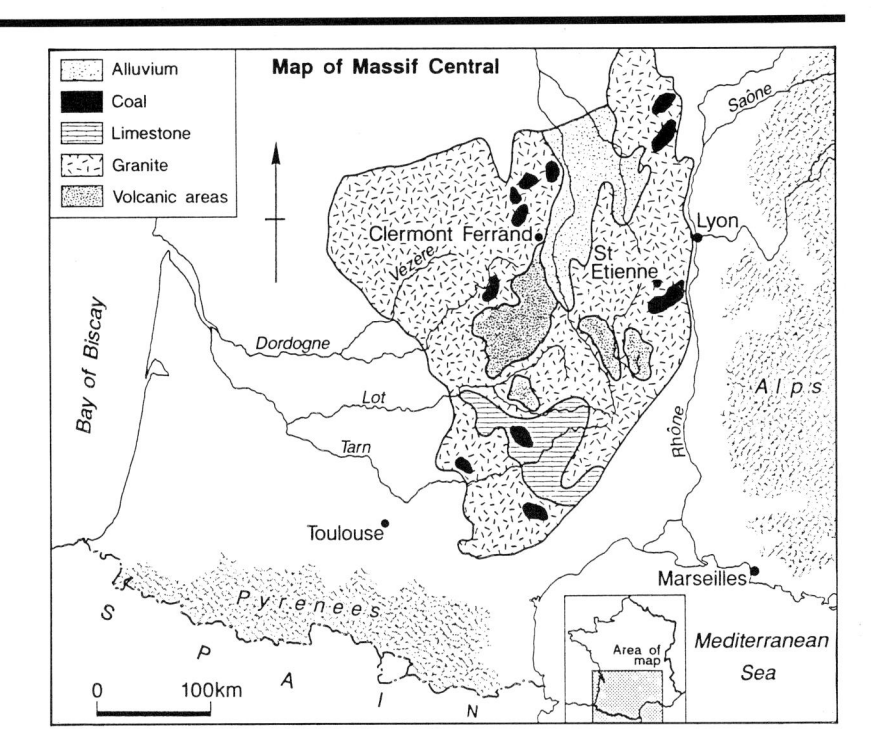

Figure 7.4

Rural depopulation

Farming and industry was **declining** in the Massif Central, so many of the younger people left the area to seek better paid jobs elsewhere – in other words the region was suffering from **rural depopulation**. This can be quite a serious problem if allowed to continue because an area can become very poor if few people are there to maintain it.

Figure 7.6

Plans to combat rural depopulation in the Massif Central

1 Improve agriculture and plant forests.
2 Promote tourism (eg skiing in winter; water sports, climbing and caving in summer).
3 Improve the quality of farming livestock in sheep and cattle breeding stations.
4 Develop hydro electric lakes for tourism – camping, water sports and caravanning.
5 Introduce light industries (e.g. plastics, household equipment, fitting for cars and planes, keys and stainless steel cutlery) to replace the old declining industries.

EIGHT

COAL AND CONSERVATION
Le charbon et la conservation

France is a rich country. The coalfields of the Nord and of the Pas de Calais (northern France) helped the country to develop into a wealthy **industrialised** nation during the nineteenth and twentieth centuries.

Coal is used to heat up iron ore and limestone in order to produce iron and steel. It was also used to power steam engines which could be used to turn the machinery for weaving cloth. As a result northern France became very important for the **coalmining** and the **iron and steel industry** and Belgium (just over the border) became important for **textiles.**

Figure 8.1

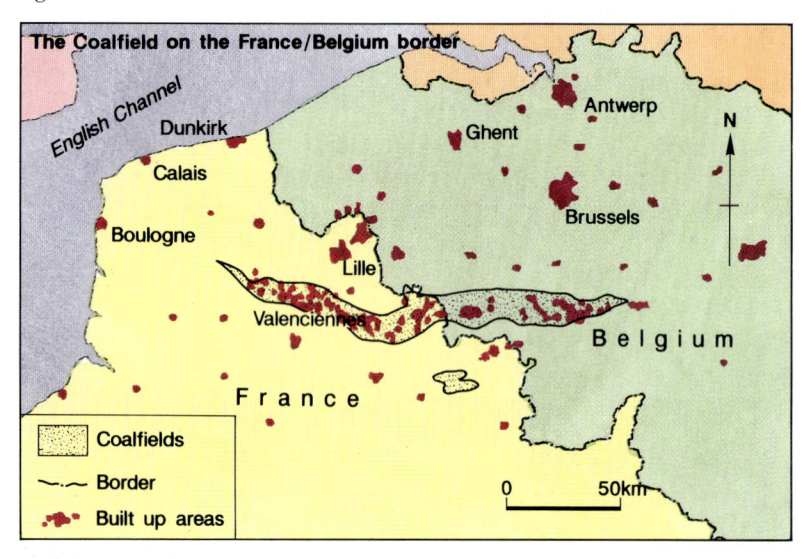

When coal is being mined much of the material dug out of the ground is waste. Often in the past the waste was piled into a heap known as a **coal tip** or **slag heap** *un terril* (see Figure 8.2).

Figure 8.2

TASK 1

1 What is coal used for? Draw a poster showing all the uses of coal.

2 Look at the map of northern France and Belgium (Figure 8.1).
a) Using the scale measure the length of the main coalfield.
b) How wide is this coalfield?

3 There are many towns situated on the actual coalfield. Why is this?

The decline of coalmining

Even though the coal of northern France was an important **resource**, its importance has gradually decreased. This is called **industrial decline.** The reasons for the decline are listed in Figure 8.3 As a result of the decline in coal mining the iron and steel industry and textiles have also been hit. Consequently northern France has suffered **environmental** problems. A list of environmental problems is shown in Figure 8.4.

Figure 8.3

> Reasons for the decline of coalmining in Northern France
> 1 Some of the coal had been 'worked out' (used up).
> 2 Coalmining methods were old fashioned.
> 3 Machinery was out of date and costly to replace.
> 4 Oil and gas imported from other countries was cheaper than coal.
> 5 Some countries (eg USA) mined coal at a cheaper price.
> 6 Some of the remaining coal was difficult to mine.

TASK 2

1 a) Look at the reasons for the decline of the coal industry (Figure 8.3). Do you think any of the problems could have been solved? Explain your answer.

b) Imagine you are a newspaper reporter living in the Nord. You have just heard that the local coal mine is to close. Write an article about the closure of the mine and the effect it will have on the local community.

2 Look at the list of environmental problems (Figure 8.4).

a) What does environment mean?

b) The word ecology is often used nowadays. What do you understand by this word?

c) All the environmental problems listed in Figure 8.4 can be solved by good management. Look at the drawing in Figure 8.5, place a piece of tracing paper over the drawing and, using it as a base, draw what you think the area could look like if it was properly managed and landscaped. (If you need help look at the list of suggestions in Figure 8.6 and you may be able to think of some more suggestions yourself). Put notes around your tracing to say what you have done and why. (Remember that all landscaping work can be costly and some things may be necessary to keep, in spite of their effect on the environment).

Figure 8.5

Figure 8.4

Environmental problems in Northern France
1 Old coal mines now derelict and dangerous.
2 Coal tips can be dangerous and ugly.
3 Old canals polluted and disused.
4 Air and water pollution from factories kills wildlife and sometimes people.
5 Poor housing and unemployment.
6 Ugly and unattractive landscape.
7 Old disused railways and shunting yards.
8 Ecology suffers.

Figure 8.6

Some possible management solutions
1 Landscaping
2 Levelling off slag heaps
3 Planting trees to shield autoroutes
4 Cleaning rivers
5 Repairing canals
6 Renovating houses
7 Demolishing old derelict buildings
8 Providing new, light industries for employment

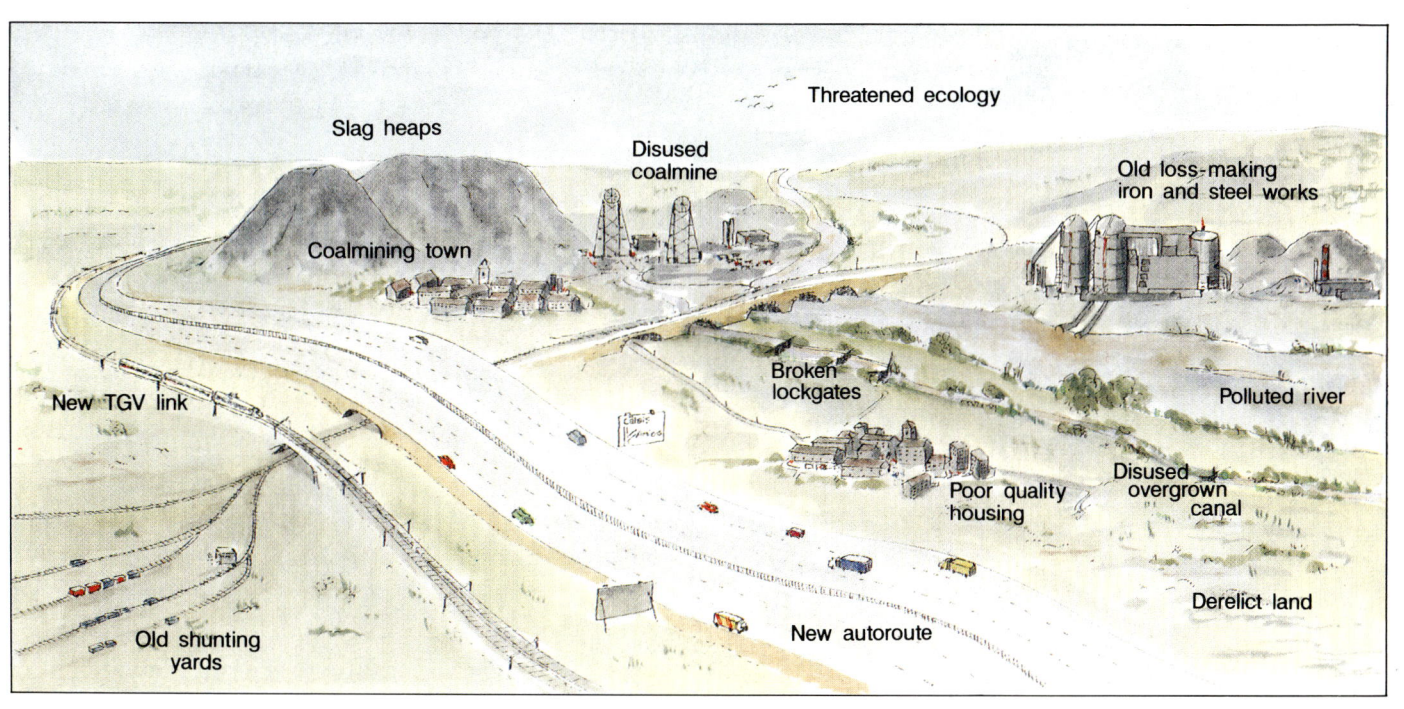

PARIS – A WORLD CITY
Une cité mondiale

Paris is the capital city and also the largest city in France. It is situated on the **River Seine**, an important river which flows into the **English Channel** *La Manche*.

The name Paris comes from the **'Parisii'** tribe who lived on the islands in the Seine over two thousand years ago. In Roman times, Paris was a little village on an island in the River Seine. The island can still be seen today and is known as *L'île de la cité*.

Figure 9.1

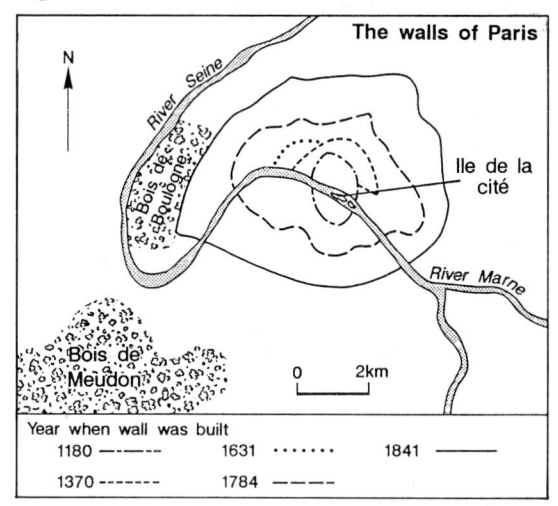

Figure 9.2

TASK 1

1 Look at the photograph in Figure 9.1. It is an aerial view of the centre of modern-day Paris. List some reasons why the island (*L'île de la Cité*) would have been a good place to build a settlement two thousand years ago.

2 Over time, as Paris grew in size, a wall was built around the city. Why do you think this was necessary? The wall had to be built five times (see Figure 9.2). Why did they have to build so many walls?

In 1850 Paris was the second city in the world to reach one million people in size (London was the only city which was bigger). Since then Paris has continued to grow and it now has a population of 8.5 million people (London was 6.76 million in 1985).

Figure 9.3

City	Population in millions
Mexico City	27.0
Sao Paulo	23.9
Tokyo	21.0
Calcutta	16.0
Bombay	15.1
New York	15.0
Shanghai	14.3
Seoul	14.1
Teheran	14.0
Rio	13.9

TASK 2

Look at the list of cities in Figure 9.3. They are the ten most populated cities in the world.
a) How many times bigger is the population of Mexico City than Paris?
b) Using an atlas find out in which countries the cities are found.
c) Draw a bar graph to show the population of each city. To do this use a vertical scale of 1cm: 2 million people. Shade a separate bar for Paris in red in order that it stands out. Give your bar graph a title.

Besides being the capital city of France, Paris is an important city in France for many other reasons as well (see Figure 9.4).

H CULTURE
J FASHION
E TOURISM
A ENTERTAINMENT
B TRADE
G GOVERNMENT
F TRANSPORT
D HOMES
C HISTORY
I INDUSTRY

Figure 9.4

TASK 3

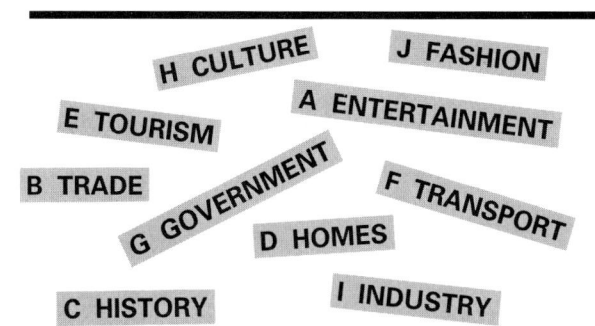

Look at the list in Figure 9.4. See if you can match the numbered pictures and French words in Figure 9.5 with the list.

Figure 9.5

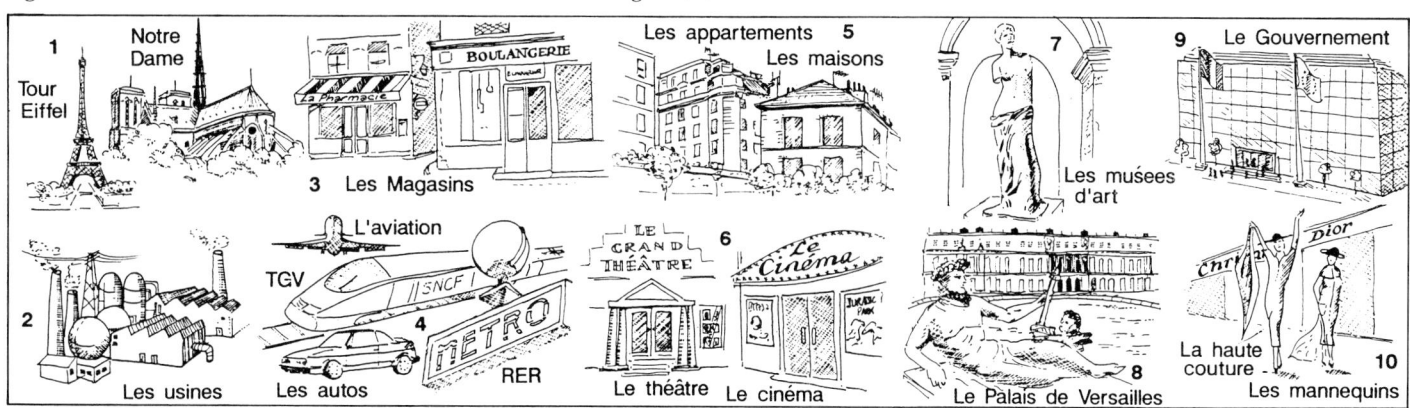

1 Tour Eiffel / Notre Dame
2 Les usines
3 Les Magasins
4 L'aviation TGV / Les autos / RER
5 Les appartements / Les maisons
6 Le théâtre / Le cinéma
7 Les musées d'art
8 Le Palais de Versailles
9 Le Gouvernement
10 La haute couture / Les mannequins

La Défense

Recently a large new development of shops and offices have been built in the west of Paris. This area is known as *La Défense*. It has some very modern buildings in it (see Figure 9.6). There are also plans to build a building here which is taller than the *Tour Eiffel*. This building will be called the *Tour Sans Fin* (see Figure 9.7), a slim glass and concrete cylindrical tower 425 m high – the world's most slender skyscraper. La Défense is connected to the centre of Paris by the *Réseau Expres Régional* (RER) which is a new express *Métro* (underground train). There are more plans to extend the RER to other parts of Paris.

Figure 9.6

Figure 9.7

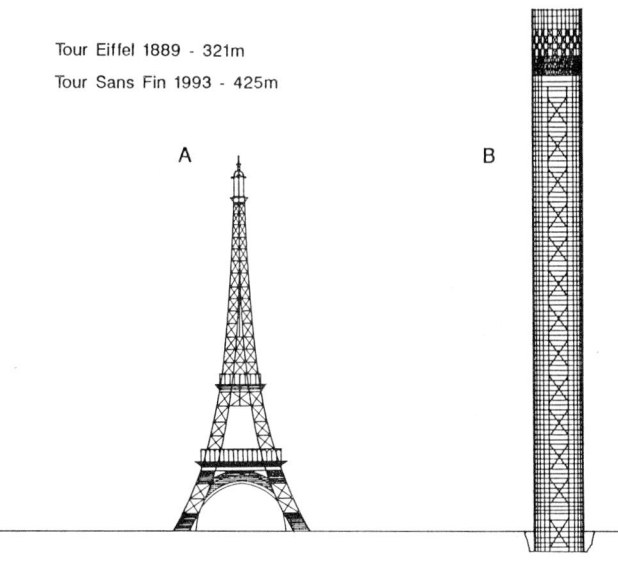

Tour Eiffel 1889 - 321m
Tour Sans Fin 1993 - 425m

A   B

TASK 4

1 What do the words *Tour Sans Fin* mean? Why do you think this name was chosen for the tall skyscraper in *La Défense?*

2 Imagine you are in the future. Draw a picture of a very modern office and shopping centre for Paris. Label the shops using French words (the list in Figure 9.5 may help you but you may add in your own French words). Label your drawing and say why you have designed it in that particular way.

The Boulevard Périphérique

Paris is famous for its **Boulevards.** These are very wide tree-lined roads, often very busy with traffic, having very wide pavements with many shops and restaurants. They were built by Baron Haussmann in 1853 under the orders of Napoleon III. There were many reasons for building the boulevards than simply to make the traffic flow better (see Figure 9.8).

The most famous boulevard is the *Champs Élysées* (Figure 9.9) which has *L'Arc de Triomphe* at one end and the Louvre at the other. However, recently a large new ring road around the city has been built which is known as the *Boulevard Périphérique* (see figure 9.10). It is a very fast and busy road with six lanes in most sections. However during the Paris rush hour parts of it often become clogged with slow-moving traffic jams. If you look at an atlas you will notice that many roads and railways **converge** on Paris. The city is known as a **nodal point** – this means that many routes connect up here like the spokes joining the hub of a bicycle wheel.

Figure 9.8

Figure 9.9

Reasons why Napoleon wanted the Boulevards built
1 The cavalry could move quickly along the wide roads to stop any attempt to overthrow Napoleon.
2 Barracks housing soldiers were built on squares alongside the boulevards.
3 The wide roads looked impressive to important foreign visitors.
4 The impressive buildings on either side of the Boulevards hid the slums which were behind them and made Paris look a very rich city.

Figure 9.10

TASK 5

1 Why do you think the *Boulevard Périphérique* was built around Paris, instead of making it go right through the centre of the city?

2 Who built the Champs Élysées and the other boulevards in Paris?

3 Why were the boulevards built?

4 See if you can find out why L'Arc de Triomphe was built?

Paris becomes overcrowded
Paris devient surpeuplé

As Paris grew in size and prosperity more and more people moved to the city from rural areas. We call this **rural-urban migration.** As well as that, the people who already lived in the city had families and so the city was gradually becoming overcrowded. In 1954, over 50 per cent of households had to share a lavatory and only 19 per cent had their own bath and shower. On the outskirts of Paris were shanty towns called *bidonvilles* (*bidon* is French for petrol can). By 1966, there were eighty-nine bidonvilles housing 40 000 people. Most often the bidonvilles were occupied by **immigrants** from other countries outside France (see Figure 9.11). However most bidonvilles have now been removed.

TASK 6

1 Look at Figure 9.11.
a) What was the total number of immigrants coming into France in 1982?
b) From which country did the largest percentage of immigrants come?
c) Look at the figures for the number of immigrants entering France in 1961, 1971, and 1981. Draw a graph to illustrate these figures.

2 a) Why do you think the shanty towns were called bidonvilles?
b) Why would immigrants be the main people to live in a bidonville?

Immigrants into France (1982)

U.K. 1%
Germany 1%
Belgium 1%
Yugoslavia 2%
Turkey 3%
Tunisia 5%
Spain 8%
Italy 9%
Morocco 12%
Portugal 21%
Algeria 22%
Others 15%

Total number of immigrants = 3.7 million (1982)
1961 = 0.47 million
1971 = 3.31 million
1981 = 4.12 million

Figure 9.11

In the 1960s the French Government tried to overcome the problem of overcrowded, poor conditions by building new housing in the form of large new estates known as *Grands Ensembles* (see Figure 9.12). However grands ensembles also had many problems after they were built (see Figure 9.13). Most recently, planned *New Towns* with proper facilities and a range of building styles have been developed such as *Évry new town* and *Marne-la-Vallée* around Paris.

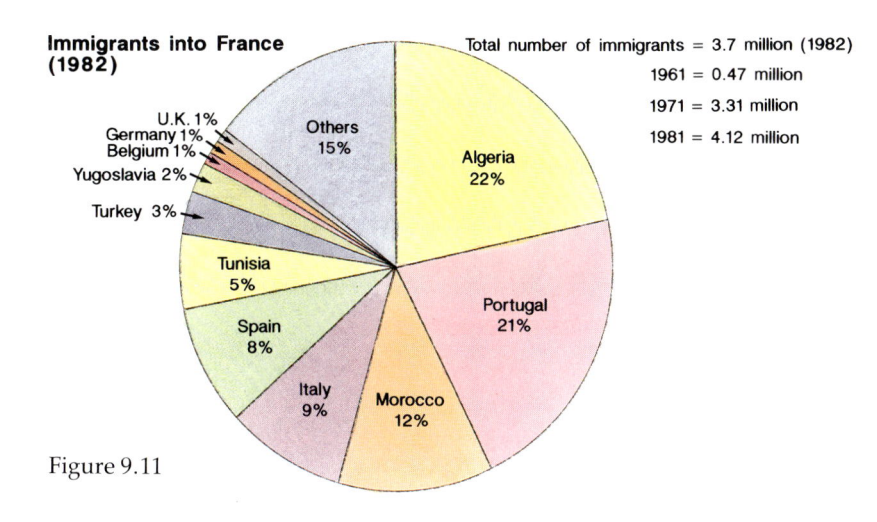

Figure 9.12

Figure 9.13

'The estates are depressing. Too many buildings look the same.'
'Our estate is too large.'
'Schools and shops were not built until later.'
'Crime is a real problem.'
'Everything was built too fast and on the cheap.'
'There's no community spirit.'
'Jobs are too far away.'
'Almost all the people living there are poor with large families.'

TASK 7

1 Look at the list of problems found in the *Grands Ensembles* in Figure 9.13. In pairs discuss how you would solve each of the problems? Note down your solutions and report them back to the class.

2 Taking into account all that you have learnt, especially the comments in Figure 9.13 about *Grands Ensembles*, map an imaginary new housing area of your own near Paris, which you think would be a good place to live in. Label your map and give it a title.

VOCABULAIRE

L'île	Island	L'usine	Factory
La cité	City	Le magasin	Shop
La tour	Tower	L'aviation	Aviation
Le réseau	Network	Le museé	Museum
La fin	End	La boulangerie	Bakers
Sans	Without	La pharmacie	Chemist
Ensemble	Together	Le périphérique	Ring road

TEN

THE SUN AND SAND OF THE SOUTH
Le soleil et le sable du Midi

The South of France
Midi-Méditérranée

The South of France is known as *Le Midi*. It is a coastal region washed by the warm waters of the **Mediterranean Sea.** The climate here is one of the most pleasant in the world. As the climate is so good, the region has become very important for tourism and relaxation.

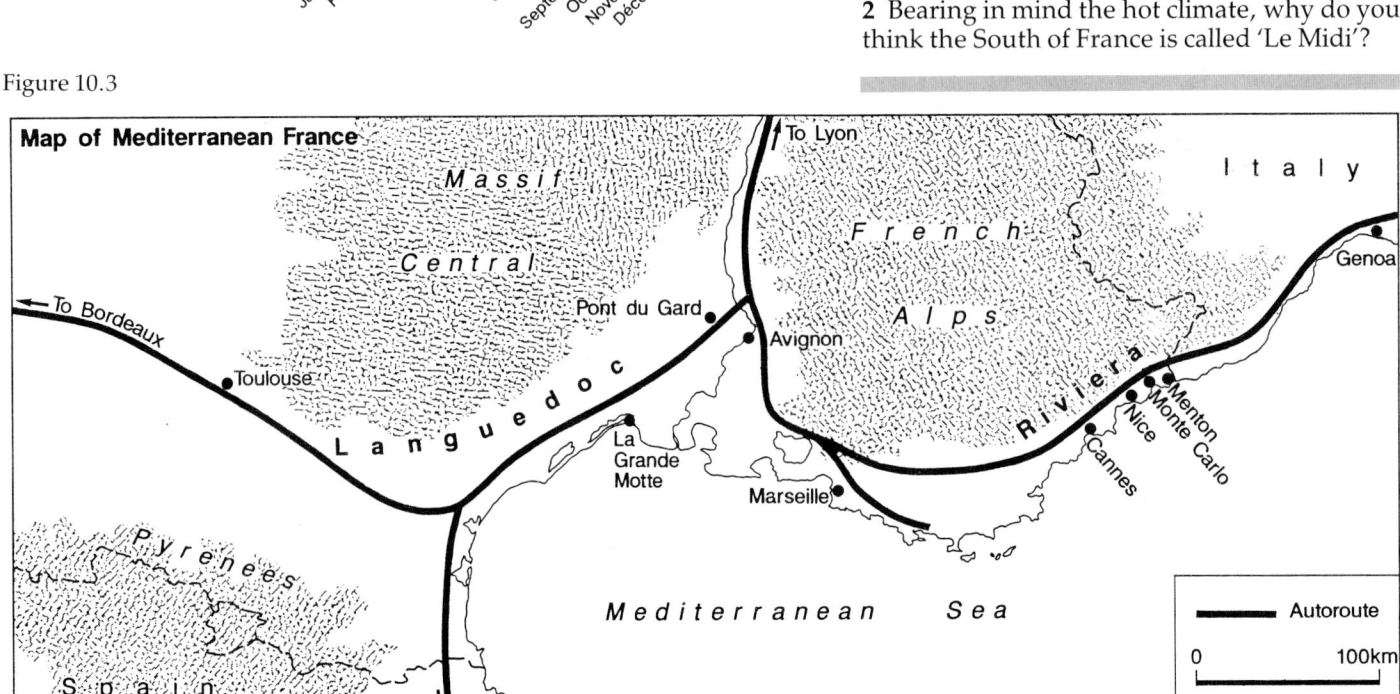

Figure 10.2

Figure 10.1

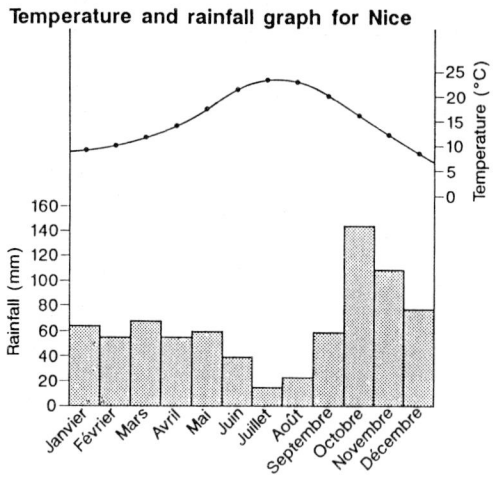

Temperature and rainfall graph for Nice

TASK 1

1 Look at the temperature and rainfall graph for Nice (Figure 10.1).
a) Name in English the hottest month and the coolest month. State their temperatures.
b) How much rainfall occurs in (i) *Juillet* and (ii) *Novembre*?
c) Calculate from the graph (i) the total yearly rainfall, and (ii) the mean monthly rainfall.
d) How many months fall (i) below the mean monthly rainfall, and (ii) above the mean monthly rainfall.

2 Bearing in mind the hot climate, why do you think the South of France is called 'Le Midi'?

Figure 10.3

Map of Mediterranean France

The French Riviera

The eastern coastal region of Le Midi is known as the *Côte D'Azur* or *Riviera* (see Figure 10.2). This is a very famous and expensive holiday resort.

TASK 2

Look at the map (see Figure 10.3).

1 Name the four main resorts situated on the *Côte D'Azur*.

2 Which EC country is situated just east of the *Côte D'Azur*?

3 Which mountain range is found north of the *Côte D'Azur*?

4 The largest French port is situated along the Mediterranean coast. Name it.

5 Using an atlas name the French island found about 150 km south-east of Cannes.

Languedoc

The western coastal region of Le Midi has been developed considerably since the 1960s. The name Languedoc comes from the French *Langue D'Oc* which means language of 'oc' – the people of this region use the word 'oc' instead of 'oui', to mean yes.

Figure 10.4

Languedoc had been an important area in Greek and Roman times and there are still some superb Roman remains to be seen, such as the *Pont du gard* (Figure 10.4) an almost perfectly preserved Roman aquaduct (a bridge which carries water). However, for a long time, Languedoc lagged behind as the rest of France developed. Even though the climate was very good there were several reasons why the region had not been developed for tourism (see Figure 10.5).

Reasons why Languedoc was unattractive to tourists before the 1970s
1 Swampy coastline of marsh and lagoons.
2 Plagued by malaria carrying mosquitoes which bred in the pools.
3 Lack of good roads for holiday traffic.
4 Poor water supply.
5 200 km of fine beaches but difficult to get to.
6 Low standard of living in the area.

Figure 10.5

1963 French development plans for Languedoc
1 Build autoroutes (motorways) to open up the coastal area for tourism for example the E4 which runs from Avignon to Barcelona in Spain and the Toulouse-Lyons autoroute.
2 Spray the coastal lakes with insecticides to kill mosquitoes.
3 Drain some lakes to stop mosquitoes breeding.
4 Plant forests to improve the dry barren landscape.
5 Improve water supplies.
6 To keep some lakes for hunting and fishing.

Figure 10.6

TASK 3

1 Look at Figure 10.5. Divide your page into three columns. In one column note down the reasons why Languedoc was not popular with tourists. In the second column note down what the French Government planned to do to solve the problems (Figure 10.6). In the third column write down any new problems which you think might occur as a result of the French Government's ideas.

2 Discuss your ideas with the rest of the class.

VOCABULAIRE			
Janvier	January	*Septembre*	September
Février	February	*Octobre*	October
Mars	March	*Novembre*	November
Avril	April	*Décembre*	December
Mai	May	*Côte*	Coastline
Juin	June	*Pont*	Bridge
Juillet	July	*Midi*	Midday
Aôut	August		

ELEVEN

POWER FOR THE PEOPLE
L'énergie pour tous

France is a highly industrialised country. It uses very large amounts of **electricity** in its industries and in the home. Figure 11.1 shows some of the different ways in which electricity can be produced.

Energy resources in France
Les ressources de l'énergie en France

Energy resources are the minerals and materials which are needed to produce energy, for example **coal, oil, gas** and **petroleum**. France has few of these energy resources (see Figure 11.2), so imports the material from other countries.

Figure 11.1

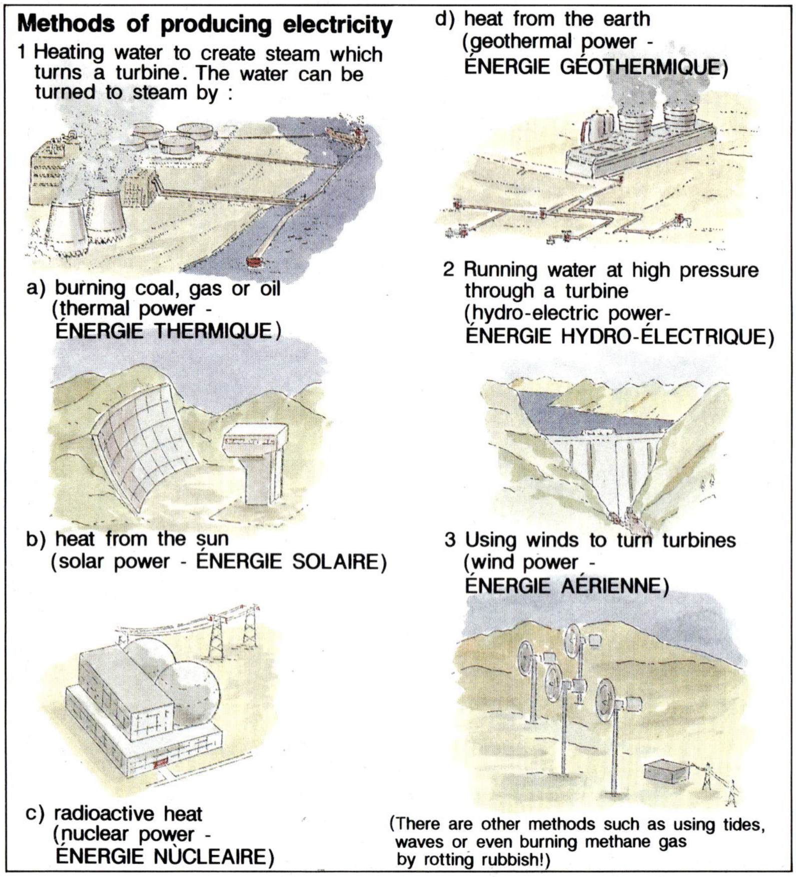

Methods of producing electricity
1 Heating water to create steam which turns a turbine. The water can be turned to steam by:
 a) burning coal, gas or oil (thermal power - ÉNERGIE THERMIQUE)
 b) heat from the sun (solar power - ÉNERGIE SOLAIRE)
 c) radioactive heat (nuclear power - ÉNERGIE NUCLEAIRE)
 d) heat from the earth (geothermal power - ÉNERGIE GÉOTHERMIQUE)

2 Running water at high pressure through a turbine (hydro-electric power- ÉNERGIE HYDRO-ÉLECTRIQUE)

3 Using winds to turn turbines (wind power - ÉNERGIE AÉRIENNE)

(There are other methods such as using tides, waves or even burning methane gas by rotting rubbish!)

Hydro electric power (HEP)

Most of the suitable places for production have now been developed, for example the Alps, the Pyrenees and the rivers Rhône, Durance, Dordogne and Isere. France also built the first tidal power station at Rance in Normandy.

Nuclear power

France is the world's largest producer of nuclear power. In 1992, it had 43 working nuclear power stations.

Coal

Over the last 200 years whilst France was growing as an industrial nation, coal played a very important part. During that time, there were several coalfields in France. Gradually, the coal began to run out, or become more difficult to mine, and a lot of coalmines were closed down.

Oil

France has a number of small oilfields, but much of the oil has to be imported, mainly from Saudi Arabia, Nigeria, Norway and the UK.

Gas

Some gas deposits are found to the south-west of France near the Spanish border. However, most gas is imported from the Netherlands, Russia, Algeria and the UK.

France needs to continue producing energy if it wishes to remain as a powerful industrial country. However all forms of energy production can have very bad **environmental effects** for example pollution, destruction of the landscape and the effect on wildlife.

TASK 1

1
a) Why did France decide to develop more nuclear power stations?
b) Where was the first tidal power station built?
c) Name the main gas deposit found in France.
d) Where does France get most of its oil from?
e) Why did the Government decide to close down most of the coalmines?

2 Look at Figure 11.3. The figures show the percentages of energy capacity of all the member countries of the EC. Convert these figures into a series of **percentage bars**.

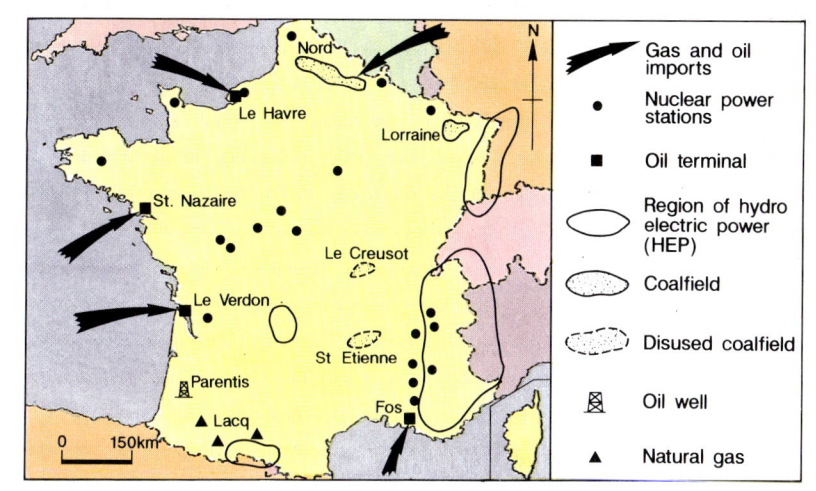

Figure 11.2

Figure 11.3
Energy capacity 1992

EC Country	Thermal	HEP	Nuclear
Belgium	52	9	39
Denmark	99		1
Eire	87	13	
France	27	25	48
Germany	77	8	15
Greece	72	28	
Italy	65	33	2
Luxembourg	9	91	
Netherlands	97		3
Portugal	51	49	
Spain	43	41	16
United Kingdom	83	6	11

TASK 2

The French Government has decided to build a new nuclear power station in the Massif Central near Clermont Ferrand.

1 Divide into five groups. Each group should be given one of the following roles to play.
a) Representatives of the French electricity corporation Electricite de France. You are keen to develop electricity cheaply, cleanly and efficiently and have great faith in the safety of nuclear power stations.
b) Representatives of the Green Party of Clermont Ferrand. You are very concerned about the dangers of nuclear power (especially since Chernobyl), and the effects on the environment. You also feel that the French people should be using less energy in their homes not more.
c) Local unemployed coalminers. You have recently lost your job because the local mines have closed down. You feel that energy from coal is the best way to solve the needs of the future (and the needs of your families).
d) Representatives from the building contractor. You will be keen to stress the number of new jobs which will be created both in building and running this power station in this area of high unemployment.
e) Members of the Clermont Ferrand Town Council. You are interested in the best option for the survival of Clermont Ferrand, a fairly large industrial town.

2 Each group should discuss their roles and prepare a two to three minute speech outlining their case. The following guidelines may be useful:
a) Where is Clermont Ferrand and the Massif Central? (atlases are needed here)
b) Should the nuclear power station be built in the Massif Central?
c) What are the advantages and disadvantages of siting the nuclear power station near Clermont Ferrand?
d) Are the group for or against the building of a nuclear power station?

3 When each group has prepared their speeches an independent chairperson should set up a public enquiry along the following lines:
a) each role should make their speech,
b) after the speeches, a general discussion should follow led by the independent chairperson,
c) finally a vote should be taken.

4 After the public enquiry write a description of all the conflicts which this issue raised and how the class voted.

TWELVE

MONEY MATTERS
L'economie Française

France is one of the richest countries in the world. Therefore it has a **high standard of living** and a fairly **strong economy**. The unit of currency in France is the **French Franc** (divided up into 100 centimes (see Figure 12.1)). The Franc is a **hard currency** which means that it can be exchanged for other currencies like British Pounds, Italian Lire or Deutsch Marks. In 1991 all the member countries were linked up to the **European Exchange Rate Mechanism** or ERM (although some countries opted out of it in 1992). This meant that if you wanted to change French Francs into British Pounds the number of Francs to the Pound were fixed (with a little allowance for the rate to change) within the ERM. The ERM is a way of keeping all the currencies in the EC fairly stable, without their values changing a great deal very suddenly. Some politicians feel that the ERM is a bad way of running the European economy.

France is a rich industrialised country so it manufactures a variety of goods. Figure 12.2 shows how France compares with the other countries of the EC.

Figure 12.1

TASK 1

1 What currency does France use?
2 What does ERM stand for?
3 Why was the ERM created by the EC?
4 Look at the statistics in Figure 12.2.
a) Draw a series of percentage bars to illustrate the figures.
b) Give the percentage bars a title.
c) Reading from your percentage bars, which country is (i) most similar to France and (ii) most different from France in terms of the structure of manufacturing?

Figure 12.2
The structure of manufacturing in the EC 1992

	Agriculture and food (%)	Textiles and clothing (%)	Machinery and metals (%)	Other (%)
France	13	7	30	50
Spain	19	8	24	49
Belgium	20	8	22	50
UK	12	6	32	50
Eire	25	4	33	38
Germany	9	4	42	45
Greece	20	25	11	44
Italy	9	13	32	46
Portugal	16	23	13	48
Denmark	22	5	23	50
Netherlands	19	3	24	52
Luxembourg	Not available			

source: the Economist Guide 1992

Imports and exports

All countries send goods to and receive goods from other countries. This is called **trade.** Goods which are manufactured within a country and then sent to another country are called **exports** and goods received from other countries are called **imports.** It is wise for any country to try and balance exports with imports. This is called the **trade balance.** If a country imports more than it exports it will have what is called a **trade deficit.** A trade deficit is not a good idea because it means the country is buying more than it is selling.

TASK 2

Look at the statistics in Figure 12.3

1 Which country in the EC did France export most goods to and import most goods from?

2 How many countries (not counting the rest of the EC and the world) did France export more goods to than it imported goods from?

3 France had a trade deficit with two countries in 1991. Name them both.

4 Draw pie charts to illustrate both sets of statistics.

French imports and exports 1991
(expressed as percentages of total trade)

Imports from	%	Exports to	%
Germany	17.8	Germany	18.6
Italy	10.9	Italy	11.0
USA	9.6	Belgium/Lux	9.0
Belgium/Lux	8.4	UK	8.9
UK	7.5	Spain	6.8
Netherlands	5.2	USA	6.4
Spain	5.1	Netherlands	5.0
Rest of EC	3.2	Rest of EC	3.7
Other parts of the world	32.3	Other parts of the world	43.4

source: France Country Report No 2 1992

Figure 12.3

Gross Domestic Product

The total value of goods produced in the course of a year is called the **gross domestic product** or GDP and it is normally expressed in millions of US dollars. This is a useful figure for comparing one country with another – the higher the figure the richer the country.

The figure for GDP can be misleading. For example take two imaginery countries A and B. Country A has a GDP of £100m whilst country B has a GDP of £50m. On the face of it country A looks wealthier than country B. However when we find out that country A has a population of 100 million people and country B has a population of 10 million people things can look very different. Country A will need to divide its £100m between 100 million people. Therefore each person gets £1m. Whereas country B will need to divide its £50m between only 10 million people – each person in country B gets £5m. We can now see that country B has more money **per head** or **per capita.**

Therefore the best way to compare Gross Domestic Product is to divide it by the population – which is called **GDP/per capita.**

TASK 3

Look at Figure 12.4.

1 Which country had the highest GDP per capita?

2 How many countries in the list are members of the EC?

3 Which EC countries are not in the top 21 richest countries?

4 Where does France rank in the top 21 richest countries?

Twenty one countries with highest GDP per capita, 1991

		$US
1	Switzerland	26136
2	Iceland	21778
3	Qatar	21773
4	Norway	19842
5	Japan	19464
6	Germany	18723
7	USA	18448
8	Luxembourg	16951
9	Denmark	16673
10	Sweden	16390
11	United Arab Emirates	16325
12	Finland	15795
13	France	15699
14	Austria	15537
15	Netherlands	14625
16	Canada	14568
17	Belgium	14348
18	Italy	13052
19	Australia	11337
20	Bahamas	11261
21	UK	10120

Figure 12.4

Eurodisney

France will undoubtably remain as one of the richest countries in the world. It has a prime position at the heart of Europe and will always attract wealth. One well-known development which has taken place was the opening of **Eurodisney** east of Paris, near Marne le Valleé on 11 April 1992 (see Figure 12.6). An RER underground link from Paris has already been built and a fast TGV rail link will open in 1994. Many tourists are expected to take in a trip to Eurodisney when they visit France. However, the numbers visiting in the first year have been below expectations and it is possible that the whole complex may lose money for some years to come.

Figure 12.5

French products

Any supermarket is bound to have a selection of French produce. Cheeses such as Brie, Roquefort and Camembert are world famous. French wines such as Beaujolais, Burgundy, Chablis and of course Champagne are regarded as some of the finest wines in the world. High quality butter and French Golden Delicious from Normandy, cauliflowers and artichokes from Bretagne and melons and asparagus from Languedoc are all commonly found in the supermarket (see Figure 12.5).

As well as a whole range of food products there are also other world-famous French companies such as Michelin, Peugeot, Citröen, Renault, L'Oréal and Christian Dior cosmetics, Hennessy Brandy and Kronenberg lager to name but a few which rank among the leading companies in the world.

TASK 4

1 Pay a visit to a supermarket and note down as many French food products as you can. See how many you found which the rest of the class did not have.

2 Collect cuttings from magazines, newspapers and brochures which advertise French goods. Put these together with food labels and create a collage of French products.

Figure 12.6